It's Not Catching

Burns & Blisters

Heinemann Library
Chicago, Illinois

Angela Royston

Designed by Dave Oakley, Arnos Design
Artwork by Tower Designs UK Ltd
Originated by Dot Gradations Ltd
Printed and bound in China
by South China Printing Company

08 07 06 05 04
10 9 8 7 6 5 4 3 2 1

**Library of Congress
Cataloging-in-Publication Data**
Royston, Angela.
  It's not catching burns and blisters / Angela
Royston.
     v. cm.
Includes bibliographical references and index.
Contents: What are burns and blisters? -- Who
gets burns and blisters? -- Hot objects -- Hot
liquids and steam -- Sunburn -- What causes
blisters? -- Inside a blister -- Damaged skin --
Treating mild burns -- Treating sunburn --
Preventing sunburn -- Treating serious burns --
Preventing accidents and blisters.
  ISBN 1-4034-4824-8 (hbk.)
  1. Burns and scalds--Juvenile literature. 2.
Blisters--Juvenile literature. [1. Burns and scalds.]
I. Title: Burns and blisters. II. Title. RD96.4.R696
2004 617.1'1--dc22
                              2003019816

Acknowledgments
The author and publishers are grateful to the
following for permission to reproduce copyright
material: pp. 4, 7, 15 Trevor Clifford; pp. 5, 19
SPL/Dr P Marazzi; p. 6 SPL/Chris Priest; p. 8
Comstock; p. 9 Getty Images/Davies & Starr; p. 10
Mica B Photography; pp. 11, 22, 24, 29 Phillip
James Photography; p. 12 Alamy/Image100; pp.
13, 14 SPL/Mark Clarke; p. 17 Mediscan; p. 20
Getty Images; p. 21 Tudor Photography; p. 23
Alamy/ Image Source; p. 25 Getty Images/
Stephanie Rausser; p. 26 Last Resort Photo Library;
p. 27 John Birdsall; p. 28 Getty Images/Brian
Stablyk.

Cover photograph reproduced with permission of
Trevor Clifford.

The publishers would like to thank David Wright
for his assistance in the preparation of this book.

Every effort has been made to contact copyright
holders of any material reproduced in this book.
Any omissions will be rectified in subsequent
printings if notice is given to the publisher.

Contents

What Are Burns and Blisters? 4

Who Gets Burns and Blisters? 6

Hot Objects 8

Hot Liquids and Steam 10

Sunburn .12

What Causes Blisters? 14

Inside a Blister 16

Damaged Skin 18

Treating Mild Burns 20

Treating Sunburn 22

Preventing Sunburn 24

Treating Serious Burns 26

Avoiding Accidents and Blisters 28

Glossary .30

More Books to Read 31

Index 32

Some words are shown in bold, **like this.** You can find out what they mean by looking in the glossary.

What Are Burns and Blisters?

A **burn** is what happens to your skin when it is hurt by something very hot. Hot objects, hot liquid, **steam,** and sunshine can all burn your skin.

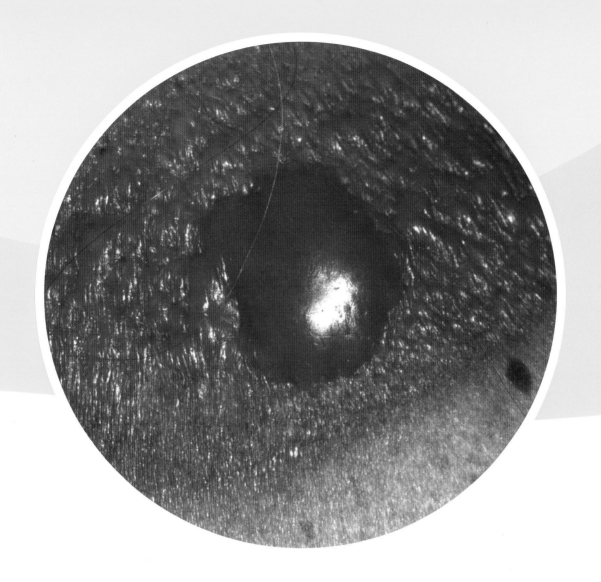

A **blister** is a bubble of liquid that forms on top of your skin when it has been burned. The blister **protects** the damaged skin below it.

Who Gets Burns and Blisters?

You cannot catch a **burn** or **blister** from someone else. Most burns are caused by **accidents** that happen at home or at work, especially when people are cooking.

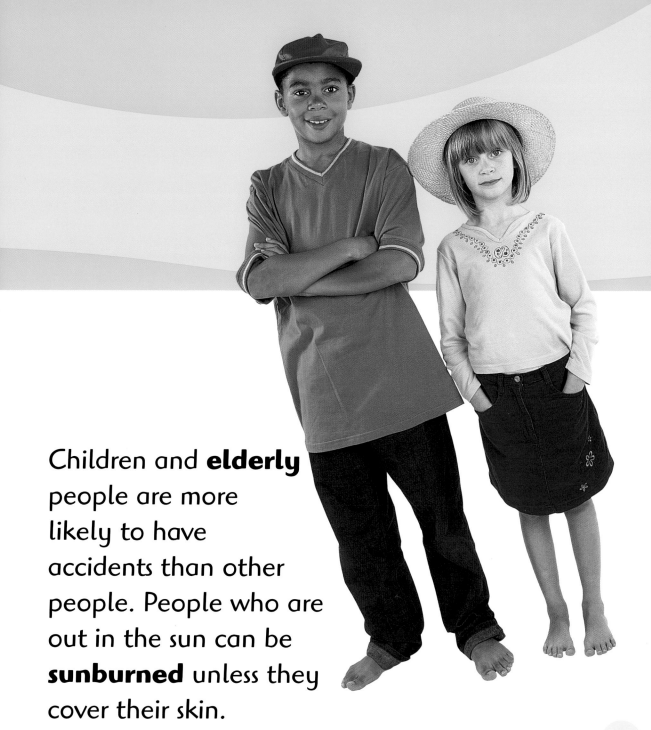

Children and **elderly** people are more likely to have accidents than other people. People who are out in the sun can be **sunburned** unless they cover their skin.

Hot Objects

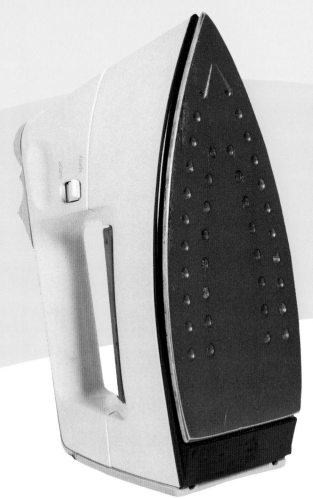

Many **electrical appliances,** such as irons, ovens, and stoves, become very hot when they are on. They can stay hot for a while after they have been turned off.

Matches, candles, fires, barbecues, and other things that are **burning** are very hot, too. If they are hot enough to burn wood and coal, they are hot enough to burn skin!

Hot Liquids and Steam

Hot liquids and **steam** can **scald** you. A scald is the same as a **burn.** A very hot bath, shower, or drink can scald you, too.

A very hot drink scalds your tongue and the inside of your mouth. Boiling water makes steam, and steam is even hotter than boiling water!

Sunburn

The sun does not feel as hot as many other things, but it can **burn** your skin. When you are busy, you may not realize that the sun is burning you.

Sunburn can happen very quickly or can take several hours. Sunburn makes your skin red. A few hours later, the burned skin feels hot and hurts to touch.

What Causes Blisters?

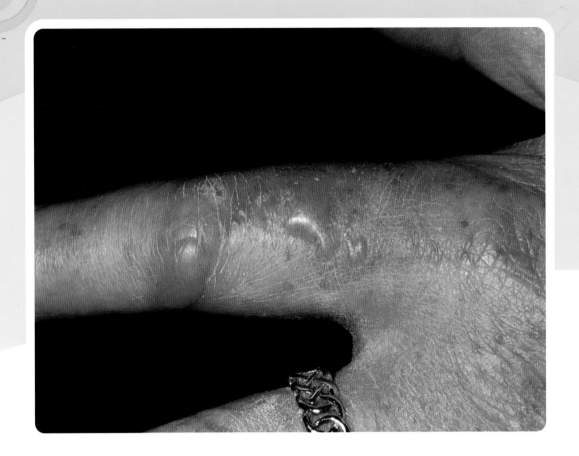

Some **blisters** are caused by **burns.**
The blister helps to protect the skin while
it **heals.** Other blisters can be caused by
something rubbing against a small patch
of your skin.

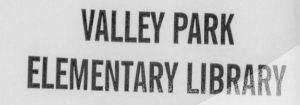

New shoes can be stiff and may rub your **heel** or another part of your foot. If your shoes are worn out, they may rub your skin, too.

15

Inside a Blister

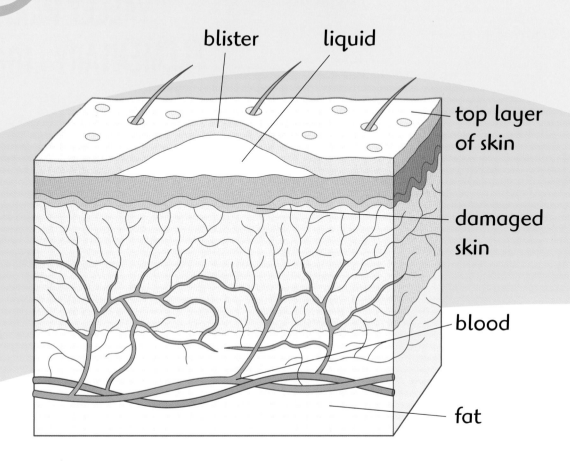

blister liquid

top layer
of skin

damaged
skin

blood

fat

A **blister** is filled with liquid that is made
by your body. The liquid forms a bubble
between the top layer of skin and the
delicate skin under it.

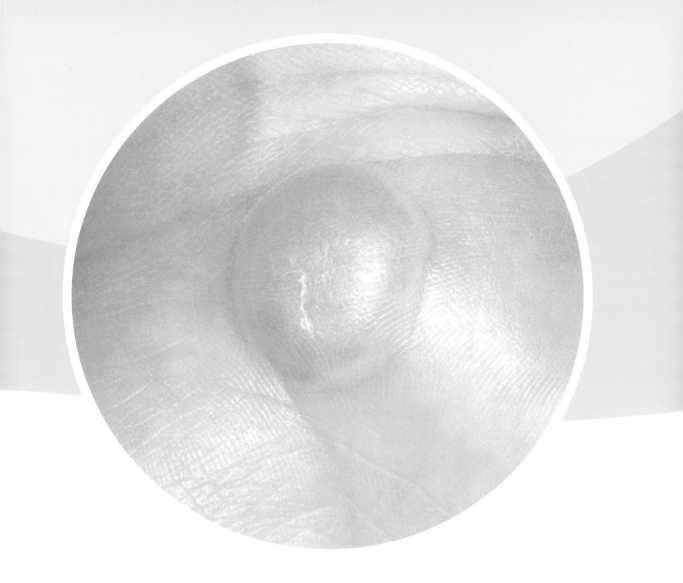

Do not pop a blister or try to burst it in other ways. As the blister **heals,** the liquid slowly drains away into your blood.

Damaged Skin

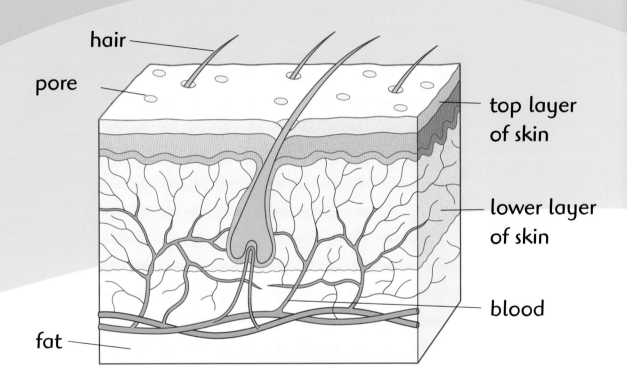

hair

pore

top layer of skin

lower layer of skin

blood

fat

Burns are painful because they hurt your skin. A deep burn that affects the lower layer of skin is more serious than one that affects just the top layer.

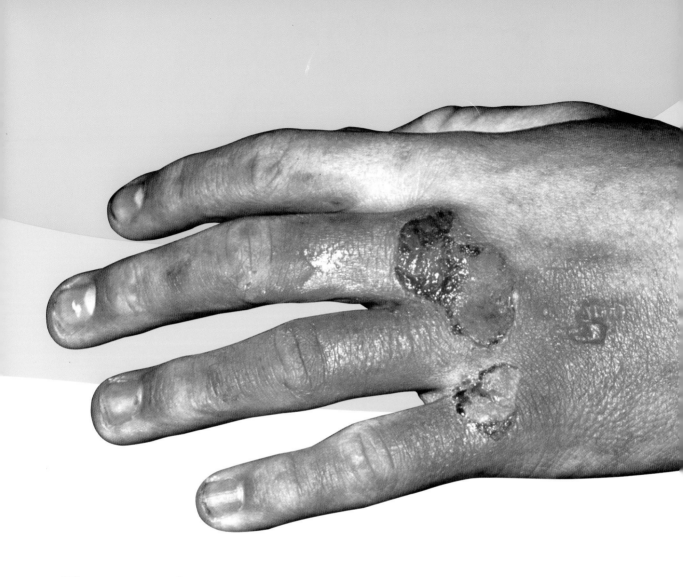

The size of the burn is important, too. Large burns are more serious than small burns. Very large burns can even kill people.

Treating Mild Burns

If your skin touches something hot, the best thing to do is to cool it quickly. Hold the burn under cold running water for several minutes until it stops hurting.

If you **burn** your mouth or tongue, drink some cold water or milk to cool your mouth down. Do not cover a mild burn with cream or with a **dressing.**

Treating Sunburn

If your skin is red and it hurts, you can rub in **after-sun cream.** This cream will prevent your skin from becoming too dry and make it feel better.

When you have been **sunburned,** you should cover your skin and keep out of the sunshine. Stay in a shady place until the **burn** has **healed.**

Preventing Sunburn

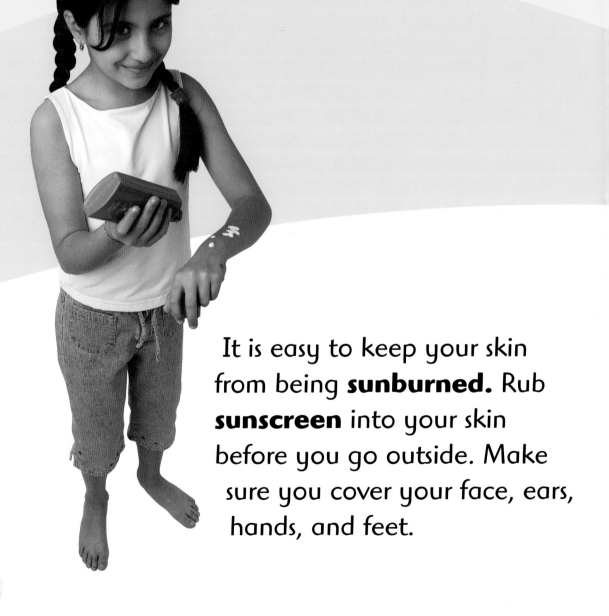

It is easy to keep your skin from being **sunburned.** Rub **sunscreen** into your skin before you go outside. Make sure you cover your face, ears, hands, and feet.

Cover your head with a hat and wear a
T-shirt. Apply more sunscreen every few
hours. Remember, swimming and sweating
washes off sunscreen.

Treating Serious Burns

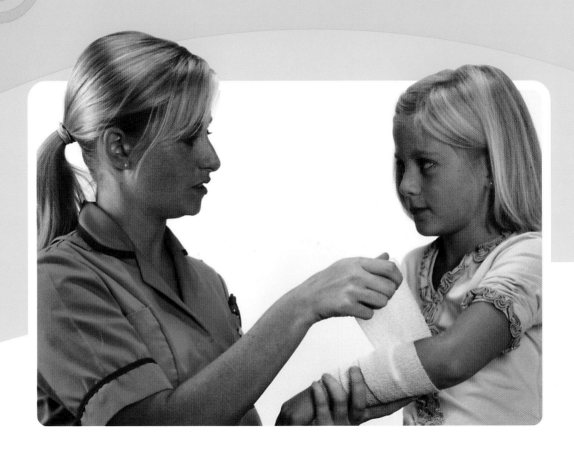

If you suffer a bad **burn,** you should go to a hospital or see a doctor. Burns can be dangerous. They can allow **germs** to get through your skin and into your body.

Bad burns can also cause your body to dry out. A doctor will put a special **dressing** on the burn. The dressing will help the burn to **heal.**

Avoiding Accidents and Blisters

Stay away from hot things such as irons, stoves, and barbecues. Remember that **electrical appliances** stay hot for a while after they have been turned off.

Avoid getting **blisters** on your feet by wearing thick socks with heavy shoes. Let your feet get used to new shoes before you wear them for a long walk.

Glossary

accident   something that happens by mistake

after-sun cream   cream that helps to make sunburned skin feel better and prevent it from drying out

blister   bubble of liquid that forms on top of the skin when it has been burned

burn   what happens to the skin when it is hurt by something very hot

dressing   clean pad of cloth that is used to cover wounds

elderly   older person

electrical appliances   machines that use electricity to work

germs   tiny living things, such as bacteria, that can cause sickness if they get inside your body

heal   when a hurt part of your body repairs itself

heel   back of the ankle joint

protect   keep safe

scald   burn with steam. Steam can be hotter than boiling water.

steam   very hot water vapor

sunburn   red, itchy, sore skin that has been burned by the sun

sunscreen   cream that stops the sun from burning your skin for a length of time

More Books to Read

Royston, Angela. *Healthy Skin*. Chicago: Heinemann Library, 2003.

Royston, Angela. *Safety First*. Chicago: Heinemann Library, 2000.

Royston, Angela. *Why Do I Get Sunburn?: And Other Questions About Skin*. Chicago: Heinemann Library, 2002.

Index

accidents 6, 7
blisters 5–6, 14–16, 17, 29
cooking 6
creams 21–22
dressings 21, 27
electrical appliances 8, 28
flames 9
germs 26
healing 14, 17, 23, 27

hospitals 26
hot liquids 4, 10, 11
scalds 10, 11
shoes 15, 29
steam 4, 10–11
sunburns 4, 7, 12–13, 22–25
sunscreens 24–25
treatments 20–21, 22–23, 26–27